Where People Live

Scott White

NATIONAL
GEOGRAPHIC
School Publishing

PICTURE CREDITS
Cover, 5 (above), 15 (above), Lonely Planet Images; 1, 2, 4 (above), 5 (below),
7 (right), 8, 9 (below), 10, 11 (all), 13 (right), 14 (above left, above right &
below right), Photolibrary.com; 4 (below), 12, 13 (left), 14 (below left),
15 (center left), APL/Corbis; 6, Jeff Greenberg/PhotoEdit, Inc.; 7 (left),
9 (above right), 15 (center right & below), Getty Images.

Produced through the worldwide resources of the National Geographic Society,
John M. Fahey, Jr., President and Chief Executive Officer; Gilbert M. Grosvenor,
Chairman of the Board; Nina D. Hoffman, Executive Vice President and President,
Books and Education Publishing Group.

PREPARED BY NATIONAL GEOGRAPHIC SCHOOL PUBLISHING
Ericka Markman, Senior Vice President and President Children's Books and
Education Publishing Group; Steve Mico, Senior Vice President and Publisher;
Marianne Hiland, Editorial Director; Lynnette Brent, Executive Editor; Michael
Murphy and Barbara Wood, Senior Editors; Bea Jackson, Design Director; David
Dumo, Art Director; Margaret Sidlowsky, Illustrations Director; Matt Wascavage,
Manager of Publishing Services; Sean Philpotts, Production Manager.

MANUFACTURING AND QUALITY MANAGEMENT
Christopher A. Liedel, Chief Financial Officer; Phillip L. Schlosser, Director;
Clifton M. Brown III, Manager.

BOOK DEVELOPMENT
Ibis for Kids Australia Pty Limited.

Published by the National Geographic Society
1145 17th Street, N.W.
Washington, D.C. 20036-4688

ISBN: 0-7922-6070-8

Third Printing 2007
Printed in China

Contents

a cold place

a hot place

4

People live in many different places.
Talk about these different places.

a wet place

a dry place

Living in Hot Places

Some people live in hot places. How do people live in these places?

People need shade in hot places.

People use fans to keep cool.

This woman's clothes help protect her from the hot sun.

Living in Cold Places

Some people live in cold places.
How do people live in these places?

These clothes help the children keep warm.

This snowplow clears a road.

This house has a fire to help people keep warm.

Living in Wet Places

Some people live in wet places.
How do people live in these places?

Some people build houses on stilts.

Some people use boats as shops.

Sometimes people use umbrellas to stay dry.

Living in Dry Places

Some people live in dry places.
How do people live in these places?

People get water from this well in the ground.

People use this water tank to catch water when it rains.

This pipe brings water from far away.

cold

cool

dry

hot

house

live

place

water

wet

Index